# OUR GREAT STATES

# WHAT'S GREAT ABOUT
# MARYLAND?

* Anita Yasuda

LERNER PUBLICATIONS * MINNEAPOLIS

# CONTENTS

## MARYLAND
## WELCOMES YOU! ✳ 4

Content Consultant: Creston Long, Associate
Professor, Salisbury University

Lerner Publications Company
A division of Lerner Publishing Group, Inc.
241 First Avenue North
Minneapolis, MN 55401 USA

For reading levels and more information, look
up this title at www.lernerbooks.com.

Main body text set in ITC Franklin Gothic Std
Book Condensed 12/15.
Typeface provided by Adobe Systems.

Library of Congress Cataloging-in-Publication
Data

Yasuda, Anita.
    What's great about Maryland / by Anita
Yasuda.
        pages cm — (Our great states)
    Includes index.
    Audience: Grades 4–6.
    ISBN 978-1-4677-3875-0 (lb : alk. paper)
  ISBN 978-1-4677-8505-1 (pb : alk. paper)
  ISBN 978-1-4677-8506-8 (eb pdf)
    1. Maryland—Juvenile literature.  I. Title.
  F181.3.Y47  2015
  975.2—dc23                    2014044099

Manufactured in the United States of America
1 - PC - 7/15/15

# MARYLAND Welcomes You!

Would you like to see giant trees and wild ponies? What about miles of coastline? Head to Maryland! Ocean City's boardwalk is the place to be in the summer. Raise your hands as the roller coaster climbs to the sky. Glide over rapids on a rafting trip. Maryland is full of historical sights and fun things to do. Lighthouses and battlefields are everywhere. There are bright cities and astounding natural vistas. There's so much to see and do in this beautiful state. Keep reading to learn about ten things that make Maryland great!

PENNSYLVANIA

McHenry

▲ Backbone Mountain (3,360 feet/ 1,024 m)

APPALACHIAN MOUNTAINS

WEST VIRGINIA

Frederick

Patapsco River

Ellicott City

Columbia

Baltimore

Germantown

Rockville

Glen Burnie

Dundalk

VIRGINIA

Potomac River

Silver Spring

Annapolis

DISTRICT OF COLUMBIA

Patuxent River

CHESAPEAKE BAY

NEW JERSEY

DELAWARE

Miles
0   10   20   30
0      20      40
Kilometers

Waldorf

Potomac River

N

Assateague Island

ATLANTIC OCEAN

Explore Maryland's coasts and all the places in between! Just turn the page to find out about the OLD LINE STATE. >

# BALTIMORE INNER HARBOR

> Baltimore is Maryland's biggest city. And it's right on the water! Watch jugglers or ride the carousel at Baltimore Inner Harbor. Try some world-famous fudge at the Fudgery. Workers sing as they make it!

Get close to the sharks at the National Aquarium. They swim right up to you in their glass tank. Giant frogs hop in the rooftop rain forest. You can watch bottlenose dolphins put on a show! You'll feel the wind on your face at a 4-D movie.

End your day at the Maryland Science Center. Touch a cloud. Play a harp with no strings. How many stars can you count in the planetarium? You'll feel as if you're floating in space!

## HARBOR ECONOMICS
Chesapeake Bay has always been important for trade. In the 1600s, it was a center of the tobacco trade. Later, Baltimore became a busy port. The harbor is still an important part of Maryland's economy. It is also used as a cruise ship terminal.

The submarine USS *Torsk* outside the National Aquarium was built in 1944 and served in World War II (1939–1945).

A wall at the Babe Ruth Birthplace Museum lists every one of the slugger's 714 home runs.

# CAMDEN YARDS AND BASEBALL MUSEUMS

> Did a ball just land outside the baseball stadium? The Baltimore Orioles must have hit another home run! Go to Camden Yards, the Orioles' stadium, before the game starts. You can watch batting practice. Sit above the outfield. Take a tour of the bull pens and the pressroom. How do reporters protect their computers from foul balls?

Explore the Babe Ruth Birthplace Museum. Babe was a famous home run hitter. His childhood catcher's mitt is on display.

The nearby Sports Legends Museum celebrates local sports heroes. The museum also celebrates champion horses and Olympians such as swimmer Michael Phelps. With jerseys and helmets to try on, anyone can pretend to be a favorite athlete! Get into a huddle. Or put yourself on a *Sports Illustrated* magazine cover. You can even play a virtual game of soccer!

## THE PIMLICO RACE COURSE

The Pimlico Race Course in Baltimore is the second-oldest horse racecourse in the United States. It holds one of the most important horse races in the world, the Preakness Stakes. This race has taken place at Pimlico every year since 1873! The winning jockey takes home $1.5 million. The winning horse wears a blanket of black-eyed Susans, the state flower.

# FORT McHENRY

> Fort McHenry is a fort and a monument built in Baltimore in the late 1700s. The fort is shaped like a giant star.

Costumed guides will present you with a wooden musket. Try on period clothes too. Help defend the fort! Discover tunnels and passageways where soldiers slept. Prisoners were kept in them too. Volunteers play drums and fifes. Plug your ears when the cannon fires! It's loud enough to make the ground shake!

Help a ranger lower the fort's giant US flag in the morning or the afternoon. It is 30 feet (9 meters) tall!

## "THE STAR-SPANGLED BANNER"

A lawyer and poet named Francis Scott Key saw the British attack Fort McHenry during the War of 1812 (1812–1815). Cannons fired for a whole night. But the American flag still flew over the fort in the morning. Key was so moved that he wrote a poem. It was later set to music. "The Star-Spangled Banner" became the country's national anthem.

It takes a whole team to lower the massive US flag at Fort McHenry.

The snow tubing course at Wisp Resort lets sledders fly downhill on tubes.

# MARYLAND
# ADVENTURE PARKS

> Get ready to get wet! Adventure Sports Center International is a rafting and rock-climbing center on a mountaintop in McHenry. Rafters can take a ride with nonstop action down a human-made river. Rafts bounce over big drops, waves, and pools.

The adventure continues back on land at the nearby Wisp Resort. It's the only ski resort in the state. Zoom down snowy hills on the snow tubing course. In the summer, fly like a bird on the zip lines! Run across a log bridge high above a safety net. It's the Chipmunk Challenge Course! Climb on swinging platforms. The resort even has a mountain roller coaster. It is full of drops and spins. You and a partner drive your own cart. You control the speed! How fast will you go?

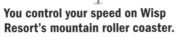

You control your speed on Wisp Resort's mountain roller coaster.

# PIRATES AND PRESIDENTS

> Ahoy, matey! Hop aboard a pirate ship in Annapolis at Pirate Adventures on the Chesapeake. Set a course for the high seas! Paint on your pirate mustache. Get a temporary mermaid or skull tattoo. Now you're ready to sail Chesapeake Bay. Keep a sharp eye out for the villain Pirate Pete. If you see him, grab hold of the water cannon. Soak the bad guy. You might even find sunken treasure.

Head back to shore. Walk the same sidewalks that George Washington and Thomas Jefferson did! Tour the US Naval Academy. Many generations of marines and navy sailors have trained there. Then share one of the famous 6-pound (3-kilogram) shakes from Chick & Ruth's Delly. The shake is big enough for a whole family.

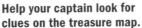

Help your captain look for clues on the treasure map.

### THE OLD LINE STATE

During the American Revolution (1775–1783), America's thirteen colonies fought Great Britain for independence. Maryland's troops, also called the Maryland Line, became known for their bravery in the Continental army. This is where Maryland's nickname, the Old Line State, came from. Annapolis became the capital of the United States of America when the war ended. The Continental Congress met in this city from November 1783 until June 1784.

# NATIONAL HARD CRAB DERBY

> The National Hard Crab Derby in Crisfield has been a hit for more than sixty-five years. Where else can you watch racing blue crabs scuttle across a finish line? This festival takes place on Labor Day weekend each year. It features food and fun. Take a seat in the bleachers for the Governor's Cup Race. Approximately four hundred crabs scramble down a wet slope to the finish. Cheer one on! Even the governor enters a crab in the race.

The festival has many games and carnival rides, including a Ferris wheel. Watch the parade down Main Street that includes marching bands, bagpipers, and colorful floats. Catch candy thrown from floats and wave to Miss Crustacean, the beauty pageant winner. Amazing fireworks finish off Sunday evening.

Young children and adults alike enjoy the Ferris wheel at the National Hard Crab Derby.

Which crab do you think will win the race?

17

Learn to tap maple trees and make maple syrup at Swallow Falls State Park.

# SWALLOW FALLS STATE PARK

> Prepare to get wet at Swallow Falls State Park! This park in western Maryland is home to four waterfalls. You will hear them before you spot them. Muddy Creek Falls is the highest waterfall with only one fall in the state. Snap a photo. The view is amazing! Wade through the knee-deep pool at Tolliver Falls. You can even crawl under this waterfall. Brrr! The water is cold!

Walk along the riverbank trail. You'll see cool rock formations. Who in your group will see the hanging rock first? This giant boulder looks as though it is balancing on tiny stones. Next, look way up at the giant hemlock trees. Some are more than three hundred years old!

The park is full of activities all year round. Visit the park in the spring for its maple syrup festival. Dig into a stack of pancakes. Yum! Check out the park's annual corn roast in September. There's always something to do at Swallow Falls.

Swallow Falls State Park completely transforms every winter.

# SAINT MARY'S CITY

> The 1600s come alive in Saint Mary's City, the state's original capital. It is a re-creation of the original settlement from the 1600s. Board a replica of the *Dove*. The ship brought colonists from England to Maryland in 1634. Can you lift the heavy anchor? Learn how colonial sailors navigated the seas.

In Saint Mary's, you'll meet costumed guides and experience life on a working plantation. Take part in a game of ringtoss or learn how to write with a quill pen. Either way, you'll feel as if you're part of colonial life.

Outside the town is Flag Ponds Nature Park. What animals lived in the Chesapeake Bay twenty million years ago? This is your chance to find out. Hunt for fossilized giant sharks and other sea creatures along the sandy beach. You might find shark or stingray teeth, turtle shells, or clams. Before shadows begin to fall, go fishing at the pier. You might catch some blue crabs for dinner!

The replica of the *Dove* ship looks just like the real one from the 1600s.

## FOSSILS

About seventeen million years ago, southern Maryland was under a shallow sea. Sea animals, such as sharks, lived here. When these animals died, they sank to the seafloor where sand covered them. They turned into fossils. Over time, sea levels changed. The seafloor rose as waters went down. What was once at the bottom of the sea became part of the shoreline and the cliffs. Scientists can see the fossils that used to be at the bottom of the sea by digging in the cliffs.

21

# OCEAN CITY BOARDWALK

> Can you smell the popcorn? A trip to Maryland would not be complete without a visit to Ocean City's 3-mile (5 km) boardwalk. Step inside the Aladin's Lamp fun house. You'll encounter shaky bridges, trick floors, genies, and more!

Back outside, watch street performers spin, dance, and juggle. Try the hot funnel cakes. Roller coasters zip around and around. Amazing sea creatures live in the Aquarium Room at the Life Saving Station Museum.

Off the boardwalk, you can play in the surf. Plus, there are special events, such as the Family Beach Olympics. You can take part in relay races. The best sand sculptors in the world come down for OC Sandfest. Watch giant sand sculptures take shape! What will you build?

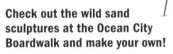

Check out the wild sand sculptures at the Ocean City Boardwalk and make your own!

# ASSATEAGUE ISLAND

Dolphins leap in the waters off Assateague Island.

> Have you ever wanted to see dolphins playing in the waves? You can at Assateague Island. It is approximately 9 miles (15 km) south of Ocean City. At the Nature Center, check out the fish tank. It has whelks and sea horses. At the touch tank, handle spider crabs, sea stars, sea cucumbers, and mussels. Don't forget to look for the corn snake!

Take a leisurely walk along the beach. Bring along sand pails to collect shells and clams. Or race a friend up a sand dune. At the top, keep an eye out for deer, birds, and brown and white wild ponies.

There are great camping sites on the island too. Don't be surprised if you have night visitors. Sometimes the ponies get curious! Be sure to check out special events like Easter egg hunts and movies under the stars.

## YOUR TOP TEN!

You've read about ten awesome things to see and do in Maryland. Now it's your turn! Think about what your Maryland top ten list would include. If you were planning a Maryland vacation, what would you like to see? Write your top ten list on a separate sheet of paper or turn your list into a booklet. You can add drawings or pictures from the Internet or magazines.

Visitors can collect empty seashells on the beach.

# MARYLAND BY MAP

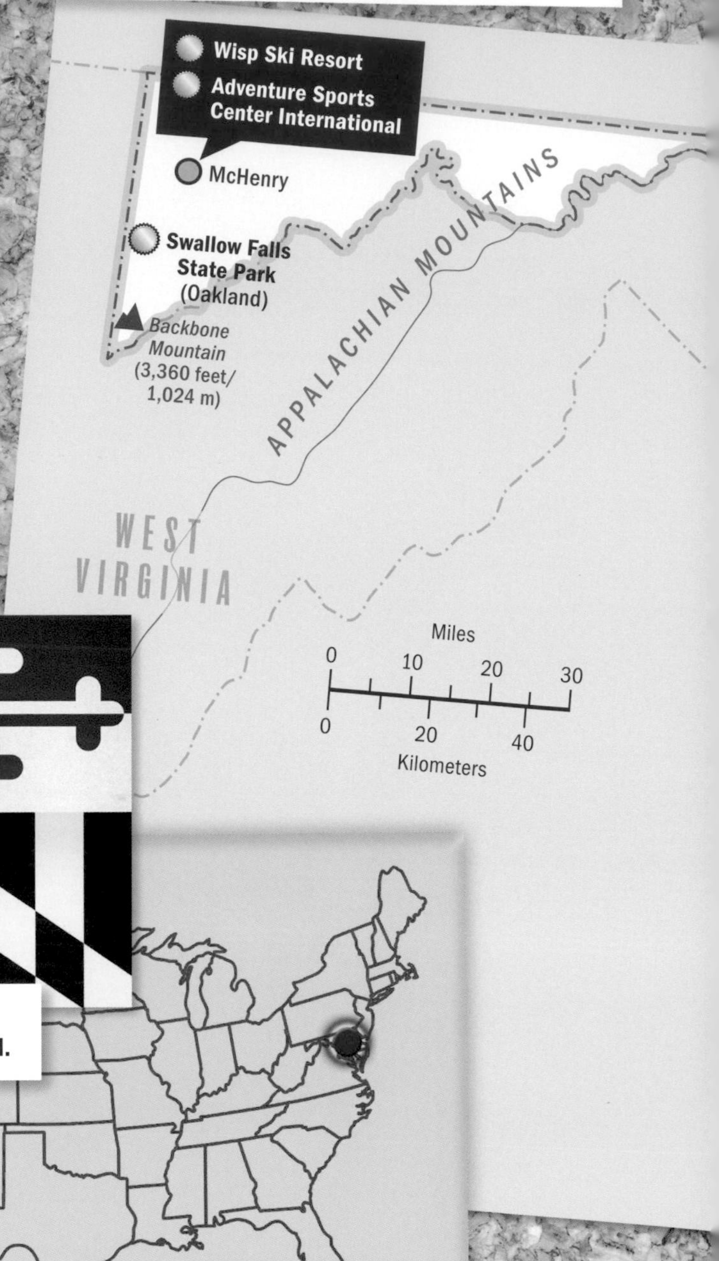

Visit www.lerneresource.com to learn more about the state flag of Maryland.

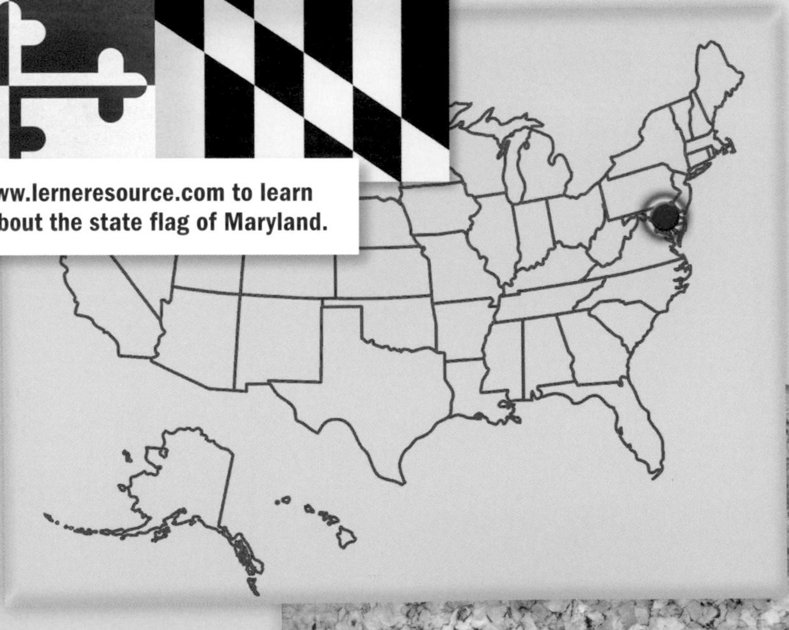

> MAP KEY

⭐ Capital city

🔴 City

◉ Point of interest

🔺 Highest elevation

–·– State border

Wisp Ski Resort

Adventure Sports Center International

McHenry

Swallow Falls State Park (Oakland)

Backbone Mountain (3,360 feet/ 1,024 m)

APPALACHIAN MOUNTAINS

WEST VIRGINIA

Miles
0    10    20    30
0    20    40
Kilometers

26

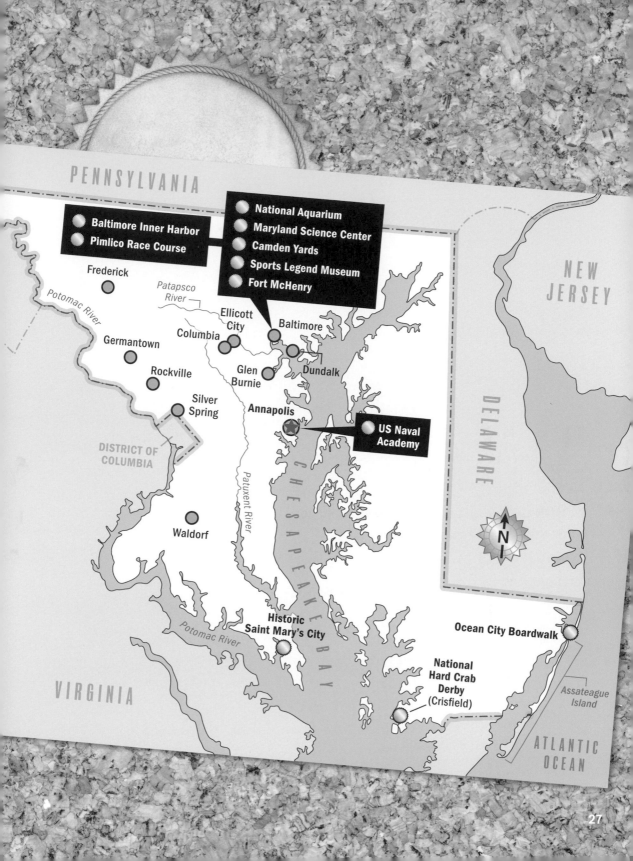

PENNSYLVANIA

NEW JERSEY

DELAWARE

**Baltimore Inner Harbor**
**Pimlico Race Course**

**National Aquarium**
**Maryland Science Center**
**Camden Yards**
**Sports Legend Museum**
**Fort McHenry**

Frederick

*Patapsco River*

*Potomac River*

Ellicott City

Columbia

Baltimore

Germantown

Glen Burnie

Dundalk

Rockville

Silver Spring

Annapolis

**US Naval Academy**

DISTRICT OF COLUMBIA

*Patuxent River*

C H E S A P E A K E   B A Y

Waldorf

*Potomac River*

**Historic Saint Mary's City**

**Ocean City Boardwalk**

**National Hard Crab Derby** (Crisfield)

*Assateague Island*

N

VIRGINIA

ATLANTIC OCEAN

# MARYLAND FACTS

**NICKNAME:** Old Line State

**SONG:** "Maryland, My Maryland" by James Ryder Randall

**MOTTO:** *Fatti maschii, parole femine*, or "Strong deeds, gentle words"

**> FLOWER:** black-eyed Susan

**TREE:** white oak

**> BIRD:** Baltimore oriole

**DOG:** Chesapeake Bay retriever

**> DESSERT:** Smith Island Cake

**DATE AND RANK OF STATEHOOD:** April 28, 1788; the 7th state

**CAPITAL:** Annapolis

**AREA:** 10,455 square miles (27,078 sq. km)

**AVERAGE JANUARY TEMPERATURE:** 33°F (1°C)

**AVERAGE JULY TEMPERATURE:** 75°F (24°C)

**POPULATION AND RANK:** 5,928,814; 19th (2013)

**MAJOR CITIES AND POPULATIONS:** Baltimore (620,961), Columbia (99,615), Germantown (86,395), Silver Spring (71,452)

**NUMBER OF US CONGRESS MEMBERS:** 8 representatives, 2 senators

**NUMBER OF ELECTORAL VOTES:** 10

**NATURAL RESOURCES:** clay, coal, crushed stone, granite, limestone, natural gas, sand and gravel, talc

**> AGRICULTURAL PRODUCTS:** barley, broiler chickens, corn, milk

**MANUFACTURED GOODS:** chemicals, computers and electronics, machinery, plastics and rubber, printed materials, transportation equipment

**HOLIDAYS AND CELEBRATIONS:** Maryland Day, Maryland State Jousting Championship, Preakness Stakes

# GLOSSARY

**anthem:** a country's song that expresses national pride

**colonial:** relating to the thirteen colonies that first made up the United States

**economy:** the money and goods a place and its people produce

**fife:** a small flute

**fossil:** the remains of an animal or plant that lived a long time ago

**harbor:** a place along a coast that is deep enough for ships to anchor

**plantation:** a large farm where crops were grown for sale, often using slave labor

**port:** a city on the water where ships stop to trade goods

**quill pen:** a writing tool made from a bird's feather

**whelk:** a large snail that lives in the water

# FURTHER INFORMATION

**Maryland Historical Society**
http://www.mdhs.org
Visit the Maryland Historical Society's website to see historical exhibitions, including paintings and photographs.

**Maryland Kids Page**
http://www.mdkidspage.org
Explore this official Maryland government site to read more about the state's history, government, and geography.

McDowell, Pamela. *Maryland: The Old Line State.* New York: Av2 by Weigl, 2013. This book is full of information about Maryland, including geography, history, and fun facts.

Spier, Peter. *The Star-Spangled Banner*. New York: Doubleday, 2014. Learn about the history of the war and the battle that inspired Francis Scott Key to write "The Star-Spangled Banner" in this illustrated history.

**Visit Maryland**
http://visitmaryland.org/Pages/MarylandHome.aspx
This is Maryland's official tourism page, with information on places to see, things to do, and events.

Walker, Sally M. *Ghost Walls: The Story of a 17th-Century Colonial Homestead*. Minneapolis: Carolrhoda Books, 2014. Learn how scientists and historians reconstructed the true story of a colonial settlement in what would become Maryland, hundreds of years after the settlement's buildings crumbled.

# INDEX

## PHOTO ACKNOWLEDGMENTS

The images in this book are used with the permission of: © Amedved/iStock/Thinkstock, p. 1; NASA, pp. 2–3; © ymn/iStock/Thinkstock, p. 4; © Laura Westlund/Independent Picture Service, pp. 5, 27; © CoastalPics/iStock/Thinkstock, p. 5; © American Spirit/Shutterstock Images, pp. 6–7; © Warren Price Photography/Shutterstock Images, p. 7; © The Protected Art Archive/Alamy, p. 6; © Heath Oldham /Shutterstock Images, pp. 8–9; © Vespasian/Alamy, p. 8; Arthur S. Siegel/Library of Congress, p. 9 (LC-DIG-fsa-8d29228); © Ron Solomon/Newscom, pp. 10–11; © Bill Manning/iStock/Thinkstock, p. 11 (bottom); Percy Moran/Library of Congress, p. 11 (top) (LC-DIG-ds-00032a); © Ammet Jack /Shutterstock Images, pp. 12–13; © Jon-Michael Sullivan/The Augusta Chronicle/ZumaPress/Alamy, p. 12; © withGod/Shutterstock Images, p. 13; © D. Trozzo/Alamy, pp. 14–15; © Sabine Lubenow /Alamy, p. 15 (top); © Glynnis Jones/Shutterstock Images, p. 15 (bottom); © Jim Lo Scalzo/European Pressphoto Agency/Newscom, pp. 16–17; © Prisma Bildagentur AG/Alamy, p. 17 (right); © Gabe Palmer/Alamy, p. 17 (left); © Lone Wolf Photos/Shutterstock Images, pp. 18–19; © Keith Kiska/iStock/Thinkstock, p. 19; © Inti St Clair/Blend Images/Newscom, p. 18; Public Domain, pp. 20–21; © Michael Ventura/Alamy, p. 21 (top); © I love photo/Shutterstock Images, p. 21 (bottom); © Lissandra Melo/Shutterstock Images, pp. 22–23; © Arena Creative/Shutterstock Images, p. 23 (right); © Sean Donohue Photo/Shutterstock Images, p. 23 (left); © Tony DE/Shutterstock Images, pp. 24–25; © Fuse/Thinkstock, p. 24; © kobps2/iStock /Thinkstock, p. 25; © nicoolay/iStockphoto, p. 26; © cvm/Shutterstock Images, p. 29 (top); © Paul Reeves Photography/Shutterstock Images, p. 29 (middle left); © Edwin Remsberg/Alamy, p. 29 (middle right); © yevgeniy11/Shutterstock Images, p. 29 (bottom).

Cover: © Town of Ocean City (sand sculpture); © SAUL LOEB/AFP/Getty Images (kayak); © Jon Bilous/Shutterstock.com (Baltimore Harbor); © Jay Baker/Maryland GovPics/flickr.com (CC BY 2.0) (horse race); © Laura Westlund/Independent Picture Service (map); © iStockphoto.com/fpm (seal); © iStockphoto.com/vicm (pushpins); © iStockphoto.com/benz190 (cork board).